HOME RUN VERBS

By Doris Fisher and D. L. Gibbs
Cover illustrated by Scott Angle
Interior illustrated by Robert Roper
Curriculum consultant: Candia Bowles, M.Ed., M.S.

Gareth Stevens
Publishing

Please visit our web site at **www.garethstevens.com**.
For a free color catalog describing Gareth Stevens Publishing's list of high-quality books, call 1-800-542-2595 (USA) or 1-800-387-3178 (Canada). Gareth Stevens Publishing's fax: 1-877-542-2596

Library of Congress Cataloging-in-Publication Data

Fisher, Doris.
    Grammar all-stars / Doris Fisher and D. L. Gibbs.
      p. cm.
    ISBN-10: 0-8368-8903-7   ISBN-13: 978-0-8368-8903-1 (lib. bdg.)
    ISBN-10: 0-8368-8910-X   ISBN-13: 978-0-8368-8910-9 (pbk.)
    1. English language—Grammar—Juvenile literature. 2. English language—Parts of speech—Juvenile literature. 3. Sports—Juvenile literature. I. Gibbs, D.L. II. Title.
    PE1112.F538   2008
    428.2—dc22   2007033840

This edition first published in 2008 by
Gareth Stevens Publishing
A Weekly Reader® Company
1 Reader's Digest Road
Pleasantville, NY 10570-7000 USA

Copyright © 2008 by Gareth Stevens, Inc.

Senior Managing Editor: Lisa M. Guidone
Senior Editor: Barbara Bakowski
Creative Director: Lisa Donovan
Senior Designer: Keith Plechaty

Printed in the United States of America

1 2 3 4 5 6 7 8 9 10 09 08 07

CONTENTS

Look for the **boldface** words on each page.
Then read the **HOME RUN HINT** that follows.

CHAPTER 1

WARMING UP

What Are Verbs?

"Hello, baseball fans. We **are** at the Play Ball Pro-Ball championship. The Newtown Knuckleballers **will play** the Sun City Sluggers for this year's Pro-Ball trophy. I **am** Buzz Star, **reporting** live for P-L-A-Y TV. My Pro-Ball kid reporter **is** Julio Ramirez. **Tell** everyone why you **are** today's kid reporter, Julio."

"I **won** the third-grade math contest at my school," **says** Julio.

"You **must know** math pretty well," **says** Buzz. "**Are** you a winner in other subjects, too?"

"My friends **call** me a math wizard," **says** Julio. "I **do** pretty well in other subjects, too … except grammar. Verbs **confuse** me. But who really **cares** about verbs?"

"**Stop** right there, Julio," **says** Buzz with a frown. "I **care** a lot about verbs. Baseball **would be** awfully dull without them."

"What **do** you **mean**?" **asks** Julio.

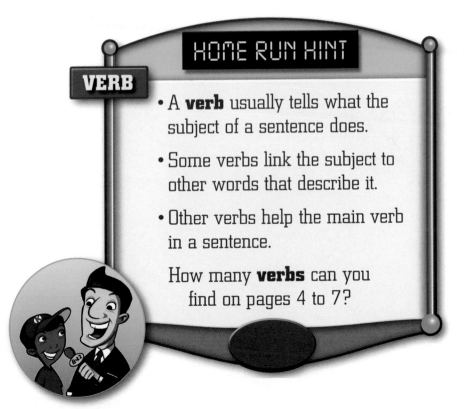

HOME RUN HINT

VERB

- A **verb** usually tells what the subject of a sentence does.

- Some verbs link the subject to other words that describe it.

- Other verbs help the main verb in a sentence.

How many **verbs** can you find on pages 4 to 7?

"Most verbs **show** action," **says** Buzz. "Baseball **needs** action! **Think** about it, Julio. **Tell** me what baseball players **do**."

"They **throw** balls," **says** Julio. "They **swing** bats. They **catch**."

Buzz **smiles**. "They **hit**. They **run**," he **says**.

Julio **giggles**. "They **slide**. They **score**."

"Exactly!" **says** Buzz. "You **know** plenty of action verbs."

HOME RUN HINT

ACTION VERB

An **action verb** tells what the subject of a sentence is doing.

RUN

SCORE

SLIDE

9

"Action verbs **are** easy," says Julio. "But some other verbs **are** *not* action words. They really throw me a curve."

"Sure, they **seem** tough," says Buzz. "But you **look** like a smart kid. You can **become** a verb champion. All you need **is** practice, just like a ballplayer."

"Thanks for the pep talk, Mr. Star," says Julio. "I **feel** a lot better about verbs now."

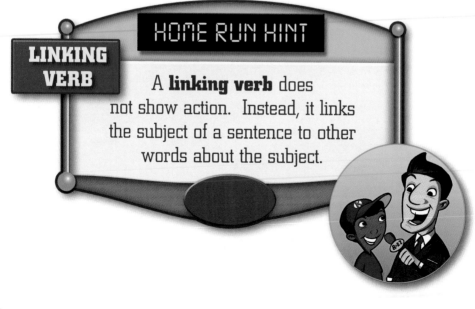

HOME RUN HINT

LINKING VERB

A **linking verb** does not show action. Instead, it links the subject of a sentence to other words about the subject.

"You **should** practice right now," says Buzz. "**Do** you see all the action on the diamond? You **can** tell the fans about it."

"I **can** see that the Knuckleballers' pitcher **is** warming up," says Julio. "The Sluggers' lead-off hitter **has** stepped into the on-deck circle. He **is** taking some practice swings."

"The game **is** starting now, and we **will** both do the play-by-play," says Buzz. "We **can** take turns announcing the action. So get ready to pitch some verbs!"

HELPING VERB

A **helping verb** comes before the main verb in a sentence to tell more about the action of the main verb.

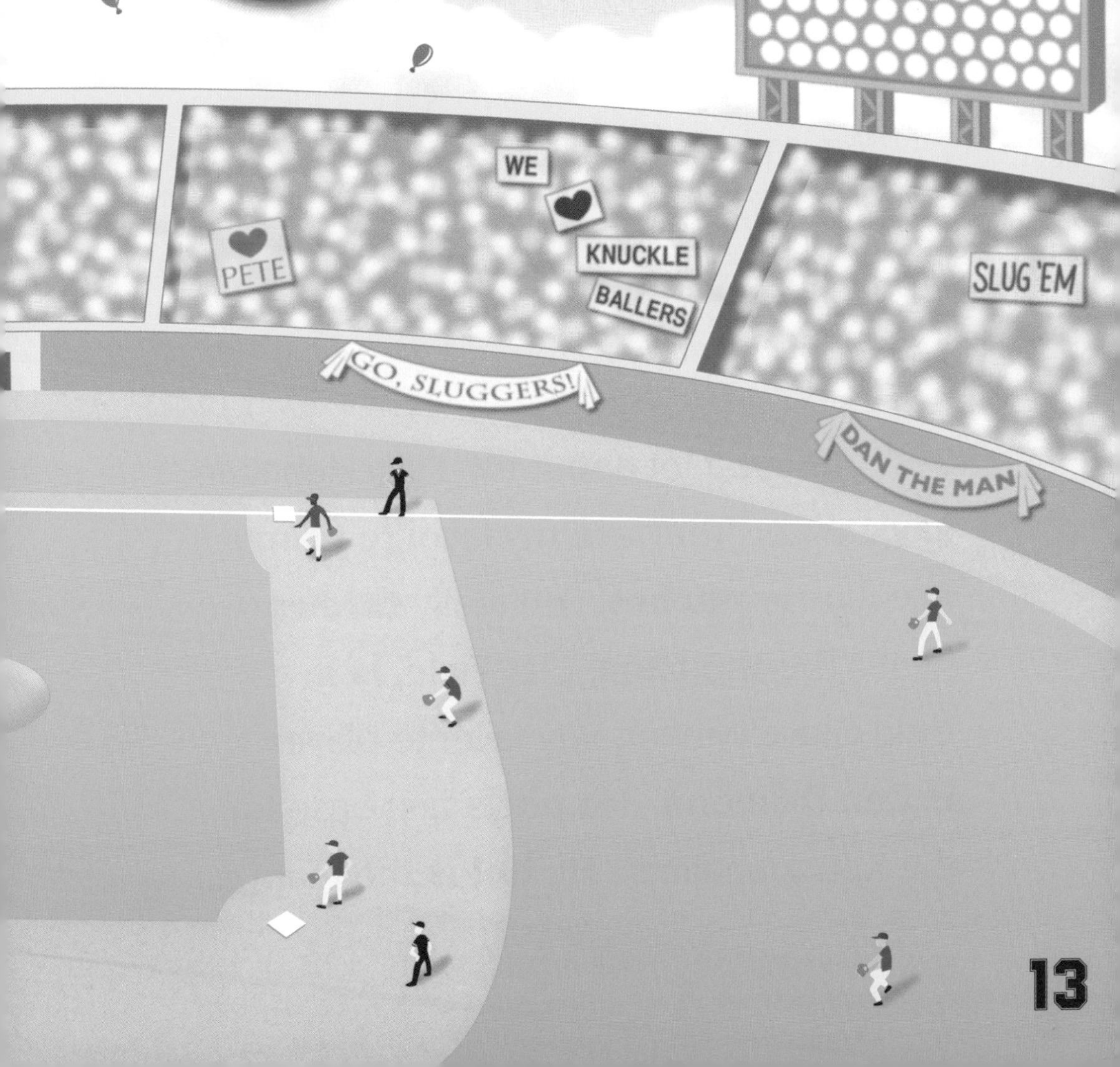

WE ♥ KNUCKLE BALLERS

♥ PETE

SLUG 'EM

GO, SLUGGERS!

DAN THE MAN

13

CHAPTER 2

IT'S TIME TO PLAY BALL!

Verb Tenses

"A good sportscaster **knows** the players and **stays** on top of the action," **says** Buzz. "What **do** you **know** about the teams that **are playing** today, Julio?"

"I **know** a lot about the Knuckleballers," **says** Julio. "They **are** my favorite team. Ace Alonso **pitches**. He really **throws** heat! The shortstop, Clay Field, **is** a Gold Glove winner. My favorite player **is** Dan Diamond. He **plays** first base for the Knuckleballers. He **holds** the team record for home runs. Right now, the Knuckleballers **are leading** the division. I **am tracking** the teams' standings."

"You **do know** a lot about baseball," says Buzz.

Julio **smiles** proudly. "Thanks, Mr. Star."

HOME RUN HINT

PRESENT TENSE

The tense of a **verb** tells when the action is happening. In the **present tense**, the action is happening now.

"How **did** you **learn** so much about the players?" asks Buzz.

"I **collected** baseball cards," says Julio. "But I **stopped** when I **joined** my school's baseball team."

"For those viewers who **tuned in** late, let's recap the action so far," says Buzz. "Ace Alonso **fired** a fastball to Hal Homer. Homer **ripped** a grounder down the first-base line. Dan Diamond **scooped** up the ball and **stepped** on the bag for the first out. Alonso **faced** two more Sluggers and **recorded** two more outs."

"Yes, he **pitched** a no-hit inning," says Julio. "He **was throwing** a good mix of fastballs and changeups."

HOME RUN HINT

PAST TENSE

In the **past tense**, the action has already happened. Many past-tense **verbs** end in **-ed**.

"Then the top of the order for the Knuckleballers **came** to the plate," Buzz says. "Sluggers pitcher Cal Cutter **took** the mound and **threw** a curveball. Clay Field **swung** hard and missed. On the next pitch, he **hit** a towering shot to the outfield. Center fielder Hugh Highfly **caught** it at the wall, and Field **was** out."

"I **saw** a play like that in last week's game," says Julio. "The center fielder **made** a leaping grab, robbing the batter of a home run."

Buzz continues his report of the first-inning action. "Pete Pickoff **got** on base with a bloop hit. Then Cutter **lost** his control and **threw** eight straight balls to the next two batters. Then, with the bases loaded, power hitter Dan Diamond stepped into the batter's box."

"I **held** my breath as the ball **left** Cutter's hand," says Julio. "It **flew** toward home plate. Diamond **swung** mightily and **made** contact. Crack! It **was** a grand slam, and the Knuckleballers **led** 4–0."

20

"**Will** we **see** you in a Pro-Ball championship someday, Julio?" asks Buzz.

"I **would like** to play ball when I grow up," says Julio. "Until then, I **will watch** every game. I **will go** to baseball camp every summer, too."

"**Will** you **watch** Ace Alonso and Cal Cutter for some tips?" asks Buzz.

"I **will be studying** them carefully," Julio replies. "Alonso **will pitch** in the Hall of Fame Game next month. He **will** probably **have** some new tricks up his sleeve. I think he **will be** the MVP."

"You are my MVP, Julio," says Buzz with a smile. "My Most Valuable Partner, that is!"

HOME RUN HINT

ACTION VERB

In the **future tense**, the action is going to happen.

CHAPTER 3

TEAMWORK

Subject-Verb Agreement

"Wow, the action in this championship game has been fast-paced," Julio **comments**.

"It **is** the bottom of the ninth, and the score **stands** at four runs apiece," says Buzz. "In the eighth inning, Sluggers third baseman Hal Homer **lived** up to his name. With the bases loaded, he **hit** a laser shot out of the stadium. My sidekick Julio **is sitting** on the edge of his seat as his favorite team **tries** to pull off a win."

"**Look**, Buzz!" Julio **says** excitedly. "Dan Diamond **hit** a line drive in the gap. The go-ahead run **is** on second base! Slim Skipper **bats** next."

"Skipper **hits** a high fly deep to left field," **says** Buzz. "Left fielder Flash Fungo **goes** back. He **is calling** for the ball as the center fielder **races** over."

HOME RUN HINT

AGREEMENT

The subject and verb in a sentence must **agree**, or work together. If the subject is **singular**, the verb must be **singular**.

"Fungo and Highfly **were** both **chasing** the ball," Alex says. "They **were** not **watching** where they **were going**, and they **ran** into each other. They **are** both OK, but they **looked** awfully silly."

"They **missed** the catch, and Diamond is on third!" says Buzz. "The fans **are cheering** wildly. The Knuckleballers **stand** on the dugout steps and **watch** Wally Wheelhouse step up to the plate."

"Here's the pitch. A swing and a miss! The fans **groan**," says Julio. "Wheelhouse digs in as his teammates **shout**: 'Pick out a good pitch!' 'Give that ball a ride!' "

"Cutter deals and … oh, what a monster hit!" Buzz shouts. "The Sluggers just **watch** that ball sail over the fence. It's a walk-off home run! The players **pour** onto the field as Diamond crosses home plate."

"The Knuckleballers **win** the championship!" says Julio happily.

"Give me a high-five, Julio," says Buzz. "You've been a great kid reporter. Would you like to cover the next Pro-Ball championship with me?"

"I'll be back next year, for sure," Julio says with a smile.

"The job is yours," says Buzz. "But right now, Math Wizard, you have some hits to tally."

BUZZ STAR PLAYS BY THE RULES!

A **verb** tells what is happening to the subject of a sentence.

 An **action verb** shows action.
Examples: pitch, hit, run, score

 A **linking verb** links the subject of the sentence to words about the subject.
Examples: Buzz Star **is** a sports announcer. Julio **feels** happy.
Some common linking verbs are **am, are, be, become, feel, is, look, seem, was**, and **were**.

 A **helping verb** comes before the main verb to tell more about the action of the main verb.
Example: Ace Alonso **has been** throwing nothing but fastballs.
The helping verbs are **am, are, be, been, being, can, could, did, do, does, had, has, have, is, may, might, must, ought, shall, should, was, were, will,** and **would**.

The **tense** of a verb tells **when** the action is happening.

 In the **present tense**, the action is happening now.
Examples: hit/hits, pitch/pitches, try/tries

In the **past tense**, the action has already happened.
Examples: pitch/pitched, score/scored, try/tried
Irregular forms do not end in **-ed**. They must be learned and memorized.
Examples: catch/caught, throw/threw, run/ran

In the **future tense**, the action is going to happen.
Examples: will pitch, will be hitting, is going to run

A verb must **agree**, or work together, with the subject of the sentence.

 If the subject is **singular**, the verb must be **singular**.
Examples: Dan Diamond **plays** first base. Hugh Highfly **is playing** in the outfield.

 If the subject is **plural**, the verb must be **plural**.
Examples: Buzz and Julio **report** the action. The Sluggers **are losing** the game.

ALL-STAR ACTIVITY

Julio wrote an article for the third-grade newsletter.
Can you find all the verbs in his article?

Last weekend, I watched the Play Ball Pro-Ball championship from the broadcast booth with Buzz Star. He is a TV sportscaster, and I helped him with the play-by-play. I talked on TV!

Before the game, I saw the players do their warm-ups. They usually stretch, throw balls, and practice their swings. Then they go back to the locker room.

Just before game time, both teams came out onto the diamond and greeted the crowd. They stood along the baselines and waved as Buzz Star announced their names. Then they went to their dugouts until the umpire shouted, "Play ball!"

Ace Alonso pitched for the Knuckleballers. Cal Cutter took the mound for the Sluggers. The Knuckleballers led 4–0 until the eighth inning. Then Hal Homer hit a grand slam and tied the score. In the bottom of the ninth, Wally Wheelhouse blasted the ball out of the park for a walk-off home run and a big win. That ball probably is still sailing through the air. It will land sometime next year!

I like the Knuckleballers, but I feel sad for the Sluggers' fans. Maybe the Sluggers will win next year. Then their fans will celebrate!

On a piece of paper, list all of the **verbs** in Julio's article.

All-Star Challenge

Look at each verb on your list.
Decide whether it is in the **present**, **past**, or **future** tense.

Turn the page to check your answers and to see how many points you scored! **31**

ANSWER KEY

Did you find enough verbs to hit a home run?

0–7 verbs: Strikeout (oops!)   **16–23** verbs: Double

8–15 verbs: Single   **24–30** verbs: HOME RUN!

VERBS

1. watched	**9.** practice	**17.** shouted	**25.** is sailing
2. is	**10.** go	**18.** play	**26.** will land
3. helped	**11.** came	**19.** pitched	**27.** like
4. talked	**12.** greeted	**20.** took	**28.** feel
5. saw	**13.** stood	**21.** led	**29.** will win
6. do	**14.** waved	**22.** hit	**30.** will celebrate
7. stretch	**15.** announced	**23.** tied	
8. throw	**16.** went	**24.** blasted	

All-Star Challenge

PRESENT TENSE		PAST TENSE		FUTURE TENSE
is	go	watched	went	will land
do	play	helped	shouted	will win
stretch	is sailing	talked	pitched	will celebrate
throw	like	saw	took	
practice	feel	came	led	
		greeted	hit	
		stood	tied	
		waved	blasted	
		announced		